The
FILMS
of
JEAN
HARLOW

The
FILMS
of
JEAN
HARLOW

by MICHAEL CONWAY
and MARK RICCI

THE CITADEL PRESS

Secaucus, New Jersey

Fourth paperbound printing, 1974
Copyright © 1965 by Michael Conway and Mark Ricci
All rights reserved
Published by Citadel Press
A division of Lyle Stuart, Inc.
120 Enterprise Ave., Secaucus, N.J. 07094
In Canada: George J. McLeod Limited
73 Bathurst St., Toronto 2B, Ontario
Manufactured in the United States of America
ISBN 0-8065-0147-2

Contents

Acknowledgments

The authors wish to extend their thanks to the following for their generous loan of photographs for this book: Carlos Clarens, Barry Feinberg, Dion McGregor, Anthony Speroni, Arthur Klaw, and the Museum of Modern Art.

JEAN HARLOW,
A Biography and Commentary

by MICHAEL CONWAY

Jean Harlow was born Harlean Carpenter on March 3, 1911 in Kansas City, Missouri. Her parents were Montclair Carpenter, a Kansas City dentist, and the former Jean Harlow. (Although Harlean did not assume her mother's maiden name until the beginning of her film work, I shall hereafter refer to her as Jean Harlow.)

She began her education at Miss Barstow's School for Girls in Kansas City, but after her parents divorced, ten-year-old Jean moved to Los Angeles with her mother. Three years later, they returned to Kansas City to be near Jean's maternal grandparents. Her mother married Marino Bello and Jean enrolled as a student at Ferry Hall in Lake Forest, Illinois.

While she was attending this school, she eloped with a young businessman, Charles F. McGrew. When the couple moved to Los Angeles, sixteen-year-old Mrs. McGrew fell in with the Hollywood crowd. A girl friend who was playing bit parts in films gave her the idea of working as an extra. Having obtained a card from the Central Casting Bureau, she found the first of her many extra jobs in a Fox film, and Harlean Carpenter McGrew became Jean Harlow. Jean's mother and stepfather were near enough to watch over and assist her then, as they did throughout her career.

It should be brought out at this point that Jean was not the usual star-struck teenager who wanted to make it big in films. She did the extra work as a lark. McGrew, however, did not particularly care for his wife's hobby. Neither did Jean's grandfather, S. D. Harlow, a wealthy real estate man in Kansas City. Jean had signed a contract in August, 1928 to appear in Hal Roach's comedy short subjects. This was a step up from extra work, but she only appeared in two productions, because her grandfather made known his disapproval of films and threatened to disinherit her. He even came to Hollywood, but his ruffled feathers were smoothed and Jean's name stayed in his will.

Jean went back to doing extra work in films, but she and McGrew dissolved their marriage in June, 1929. She got a small role and her first billing in Paramount's *Saturday Night Kid*, after which she went back to playing bits for a short time. (See the summary of Jean's early work for titles of films she appeared in.)

Whether she wanted it or not, Jean's big break came. Howard Hughes was producing a three-million-dollar film, *Hell's Angels*, about air warfare during the first World War. Greta Nissen had been signed for the female lead as the lascivious Helen, but her Swedish accent was not suited to this film, and Hughes was looking for a replacement. Jean met Hughes, and he placed her under contract to his Caddo Company and gave her the part of Helen.

Hell's Angels is today regarded as a classic. Although the critics of the day considered the film to be superior technically, they found the acting inadequate and could not accept the three leading players as British. Still, it should be remembered that all film actors had suddenly been confronted with the sound medium and were working at a disadvantage. Many silent film stars faded into oblivion, while stage actors were becoming the new stars in Hollywood.

Jean was singled out by some critics for a particular blast; yet, despite the adverse criticism, she achieved immediate fame. The public was less concerned with her acting ability because she had what few others did — star quality. Star quality may seem to be an expression that only fan magazines use, but it is meaningful in many cases. Marilyn Monroe had this quality and she was a big hit with the public because of it, even when she had small roles in films.

Films about gangsters and the prohibition era were growing in popularity. When *Little Caesar* was released, it was an immediate hit. Every studio got on the bandwagon, and when Howard Hughes lent Jean to other studios, she appeared first as a good bad girl in M-G-M's *The Secret Six*. Because Jean was able to show some softness in her part, her performance was better. Billed seventh in the cast was Clark Gable, who was to work again with Jean a year and a half later, when he reached stardom.

Jean's second loan-out was to Universal for *Iron Man*, starring Lew Ayres, who was a big name because of his performance in

All Quiet on the Western Front. (Ayres later became the movies' Dr. Kildare.) Critics liked the film as well as the performances of Ayres and Robert Armstrong, but they did not like Jean; her portrayal of a vicious wife seemed somewhat stiff and overacted, as did her performance in the third loan-out release, Warner Bros.' *The Public Enemy*.

I was not yet born when this film was made, and by the time I was out of my teens and able to go to a New York City theater which showed reissues, these old films were on television. Many people who had seen Jean's movies when they opened in theaters had been telling me how wonderful she was, so when *The Public Enemy* was scheduled for its first television showing, I was anxious to see this much-praised actress. While I watched it I marvelled at the film's fast pace and James Cagney's great performance. The next day, however, I commented to a friend that I thought Miss Harlow was an awful actress. Only when I saw her later performances did I realize that I had made a quick judgment and an inaccurate one.

Jean's fourth loan-out release was Fox's *Goldie*, in which she played another nasty woman; two releases for Columbia followed, *Platinum Blonde* and *Three Wise Girls*. The title *Platinum Blonde* suited the color of Jean's hair but not the plot of the film. In this movie, Loretta Young got the sympathetic role and Robert Williams received the critical kudos. In *Three Wise Girls* Jean played the part of a lamb in the big city jungle, but this time she played just too good a girl. She had not yet found her forte.

Her next film was M-G-M's *The Beast of the City*. She had wanted very much to be released from her contract with the Caddo Company; Howard Hughes had not given her another part in his productions, and she could not develop her ability by being shuttled from one studio to another. These studios, understandably, had no time to help Jean develop technique in the short time she worked for each of them. Jean and Hughes did agree to terminate her contract and Jean signed with Metro-Goldwyn-Mayer, the studio that was to produce all her future films. The Metro-Harlow combination proved a splendid match. M-G-M now had the time to bring out both Jean's talents as a comedienne and her innate dramatic ability. The studio was also wise enough to let Jean Harlow be Jean Harlow.

Those who may have put Jean Harlow aside as an insensitive, coarse blonde should look into her performances. In her early films she had to play completely unsympathetic characters. The critics generally found her acting faulty because she simply did not know how to play this type of role. Had she been coarse and cruel in nature, it seems likely that she would have done a much better job in these films. As for the good reviews for her role in *The Beast of the City*, it should be remembered that M-G-M was trying to build up her career and was coaching her, as they did other players who they hoped would stay with the studio for a long time.

Jean's lead in M-G-M's *Red-Headed Woman* was the turning point in her career. The character she had to play was an unpleasant one, but she did what few other actresses could do with such a part; she transformed an evil woman into a comedy character. (Her hair was dyed for this film, but she went back to blonde after it, at least for a few years.) Her co-star, Chester Morris, was later typed because of his leading role in the *Boston Blackie* detective series, and he had a hard time convincing producers that the public would accept him in roles other than that of Boston Blackie. A most competent actor, Morris eventually succeeded. Beginning with this film, Jean was also typed, but her situation was a little different. The critics — not the viewing public — were first to type her as a comedienne and, as it turned out, to help her career by doing so. At last, Jean had found her forte — comedy.

In July, 1932, a month after *Red-Headed Woman* was released, Jean married Paul Bern. Bern was one of the right-hand men of Irving Thalberg, production executive at M-G-M. A few months after the marriage, Bern committed suicide. The note he left for Jean ended with the statement, "You understand last night was only a comedy." What happened on that last night caused a great deal of speculation then, and still does now. If any reader expects to see details of Miss Harlow's marriages revealed here, he will be disappointed. Nor am I going to mention amours ascribed to her by other people, for trying

to judge a person by romances seems to me meaningless as well as foolish. Bern's death was an unfortunate incident, but I do not wish to add my two cents' worth of analysis to such a tragic occurrence.

Jean had been working on *Red Dust* when Bern died. When the film was released in November of the same year, it definitely established the Harlow image. Behind the hard-boiled outward shell of Jean's Vantine there existed a girl of tenderness and sensitivity. Richard Watts, Jr., film critic for the *New York Herald Tribune* who disliked Jean's earlier acting, praised her for her performance. (In the future, he would be one of Jean's foremost supporters.) The particular spark of feeling that Jean exhibited in this film remained in all her future work and made her one of the most popular actresses in screen history.

Hold Your Man again teamed Jean with Clark Gable, who made more films with her than did any other actor. It was now 1933. In the month of September, Jean married Harold G. Rosson, a cameraman at M-G-M who photographed four of her films, *Red-Headed Woman*, *Red Dust*, *Hold Your Man*, and *Bombshell*.

Bombshell, in my opinion, is one of the best satires on Hollywood ever made. Jean was fine as the wise-cracking movie star who yearned for a cultured, refined existence. Here I saw what seemed to me to be the true Jean Harlow — tough but kind, volatile but sympathetic, a girl who was able to take care of herself.

Dinner at Eight was officially released after *Bombshell,* although in some areas it played before it. *Dinner at Eight* is so well known and appreciated that it needs no further recommendation from this writer. Jean made a sympathetic figure of the half-comic, half-tragic Kitty. When Kitty first appears, she is a crude creature; Kitty is angry at her husband for trying to drive their dinner host out of business. She feels that his action will spoil her chances for entering high society; but more than anything else, she is angry because she feels her hostess has invited her to the dinner out of friendliness. Kitty even threatens to expose her husband's activities if he persists in trying to ruin the lives of her dinner hosts, because she thinks "they're nice people." In truth, however, the hostess is concerned only with the success of the dinner and Jean makes Kitty, instead of the hostess, emerge as the kind person.

Her next film was *The Girl From Missouri,* a slightly risqué comedy like *Bombshell,* and just as endearing. An excellent comedy, it was the type of film that only Jean Harlow could do. In another actress's hands, the character that she played would have seemed too unbelievable.

Reckless was Jean's first 1935 release. She was cast as a musical comedy star. Jean was not really much of a dancer, however, and she certainly was no singer. True, she did warble some tunes in a few of her films, but this does not mean she was an accomplished singer — dubbing is a common practice in musical films. As for the singing in *Reckless,* I will repeat the words of *New York American* film critic Regina Crewe, who said in her review of this film that Jean "acquits herself right nobly, even when she is presumed to sing." By now, most critics liked Jean so much that it did not matter whether she sang all her own songs or not.

In 1934, Jean had divorced Harold Rosson without any sensational publicity. She began dating William Powell, whom she later planned to marry.

The lively adventure film *China Seas* was another Harlow triumph. Co-starring with Clark Gable, Jean played the same type of character she played in *Red Dust. Riffraff* followed, co-starring Spencer Tracy. It was more drama than comedy, but Jean still managed to get off some witty lines.

Jean's first 1936 release was *Wife vs. Secretary.* It was a "woman's picture" — that is, a soap opera. M-G-M had three of its top stars in the leading roles and everyone expected a superb comedy. The critics were disappointed with Jean's role as an average working girl. They wanted her in comedy, but the film was not designed to be a comedy. Nor was Jean's next film; *Suzy* is an interesting spy story, but not a comedy. The film critics were therefore delighted when *Libeled Lady* was released. Jean was in her element again and better than ever.

Another comedy, *Personal Property*, co-starring Robert Taylor, was released on March 13, 1937. Jean, however, seemed to be showing signs of ill health, and she became quite ill while working on her next film, *Saratoga*. Nevertheless, she continued reporting for work, for that's the way Jean was; she had fortitude — something her detractors should remember. *Saratoga* was near completion when Jean's condition became so severe that she had to be taken home from the studio.

By the time efforts were made to do something about the uremic poisoning in her system, it was too late. A cerebral oedema ended her short life. At the Good Samaritan Hospital in Los Angeles, Jean Harlow died on June 7, 1937, at the age of twenty-six.

At first, M-G-M did not know what to do about the uncompleted *Saratoga*, but they eventually decided to use a double (Mary Dees) for longshots of scenes in which Jean was supposed to appear. This was done quite skillfully, and only film buffs might have known which scenes these were. *Saratoga* was thus released.

I can remember several mentions of Jean Harlow on television interview shows a few years back. Of all the people who knew or worked in films with her, no one ever spoke of her except with warmth and genuine affection. They did not have to do this. Many years had passed since Jean's death and they could have gained some publicity by speaking ill of her. That they did not should be some indication of how much she was liked.

Lately, Jean Harlow has been the target of adverse criticism. The many people who knew her and have come to her defense would not have come forth if Jean had been only a cheap blonde. To be sure, she had her faults like any other human being, but she also must have had some wonderful qualities for so many people to still care enough to defend her.

It seems strange that Jean Harlow's personal life should be of such interest after so many years. After all, she did not precipitate any world crises. At any rate, one good thing may come out of all this controversy about her; people may go to see her films again and see a talented comedienne in action. Two years ago, the audience for this book would have been small, because too many people had forgotten Jean Harlow. Now, perhaps, filmgoers will try to see all her films again and to judge her acting for themselves.

A Harlow Gallery

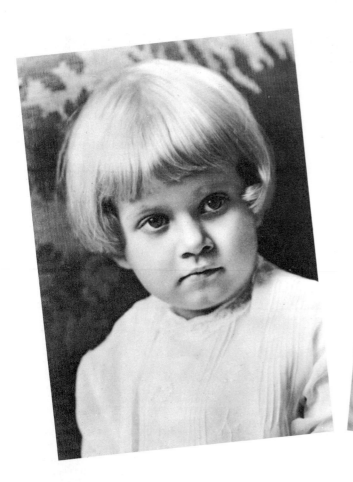

A HARLOW GALLERY   17

The
FILMS
of
JEAN
HARLOW

Stan Laurel, Jean Harlow, Oliver Hardy in *Double Whoopee*—Hal Roach (1928)

JEAN HARLOW'S Early Film Work
Scenes from *"Double Whoopee"*

Jean Harlow's earliest performance in films was as an extra. (An extra is a person who appears in a scene, generally as part of a group.) Unfortunately, it is impossible to compile a complete list of all Jean's extra work; she could have been used in that capacity by all the studios existing in the period 1928-30. Usually, the only way to tell if Jean was in a film, is to catch a glimpse of her in some scene.

Jean's first appearance was in a Fox film, the title of which we have not been able to learn. We do know that she appeared in *Moran of the Marines*, a 1928 Paramount silent film with Richard Dix and Ruth Elder in the leading roles. Also in 1928, Jean appeared in two silent Hal Roach comedy short subjects, *Double Whoopee* and *The Unkissed Man*, both starring Stan Laurel and Oliver Hardy. Her parts in these were more on the order of featured bits, which means that she had some incidental connection with the story.

Jean Harlow (seated at a table at the far left) in *City Lights*, Charles Chaplin—United Artists (1931)

and *"City Lights"*

After these two films, Jean went back to extra work. In this capacity, she appeared in *Close Harmony*, a 1929 Paramount sound film with Charles "Buddy" Rogers and Nancy Carroll, *New York Nights*, a 1929 United Artists sound film with Norma Talmadge and Gilbert Roland, *Love Parade*, a 1929 Paramount sound film with Maurice Chevalier and Jeanette MacDonald, and in Charles Chaplin's silent film for United Artists, *City Lights*, not released until 1931.

The biggest role Jean had before *Hell's Angels* was in the 1929 Paramount sound film, *The Saturday Night Kid* (which is covered separately in this book). After this film, Jean went to work for Al Christie, who produced comedy shorts for Paramount, and she appeared in *Weak But Willing*. Her starring role in *Hell's Angels* came some time after this.

The
Saturday Night
Kid

With Leone Lane, Jean Arthur, and Clara Bow

A Paramount Picture (October 26, 1929)

CAST

Clara Bow, James Hall, Jean Arthur, Charles Sellon, Ethel Wales, Frank Ross, Edna May Oliver, Hyman Meyer, Eddie Dunn, Leone Lane, Jean Harlow.

CREDITS

Directed by Edward Sutherland. Scenario by Lloyd Corrigan and Ethel Doherty. Based on the play "Love 'Em and Leave 'Em" by George Abbott and John V. A. Weaver. Dialogue by Lloyd Corrigan and Edward Paramore, Jr. Photography by Harry Fishback. Edited by Jane Loring.

SYNOPSIS

Mayme (Clara Bow) and her sister Janie (Jean Arthur) work as salesgirls in Ginsberg's Department Store. Jean Harlow has the role of Hazel, a salesgirl in the same store. Mayme is in love with Bill (James Hall), a clerk, but Janie tries to steal him away.

As treasurer of the Employees' Welfare Club pageant, Janie gets into trouble because she uses the club money to make a bet on the horse races. She tells her sister about her predicament, and Mayme goes to Janie's bookie and wins the money back

in a dice game. However, Janie has been asked for the club money and she falsely accuses Mayme of taking it. Mayme returns with the money and learns that Bill has sold his radio to help pay back the loss. She tells off her ungrateful sister. Hearing the truth, Bill rejects Janie and plans marriage with Mayme.

Although Jean Harlow's name was not mentioned in the opening credits, she had eleventh billing in the cast at the end of the film. This was the only time she received billing before *Hell's Angels*. As mentioned in the summary of her early work, Jean did other work after this film and did not go immediately into *Hell's Angels*.

The date in parentheses above is the official release date of the film.

The official release date will be used throughout this book for each film.

What the critics said about

THE SATURDAY NIGHT KID

Richard Watts, Jr.
New York Herald Tribune
   Miss Clara Bow's newest vehicle is a screen adaptation of that amusing play of several seasons ago, *Love 'Em and Leave 'Em.* It is, in the present version, considerably less than a masterpiece: yet, as a result of some amusing department store scenes and excellent performances by Miss Bow, Miss Jean Arthur and Miss Edna May Oliver, it becomes an unostentatious, but reasonably pleasant entertainment.

With Clara Bow and Jean Arthur

With James Hall and Ben Lyon

Hell's Angels

With Ben Lyon, James Hall, and Evelyn Hall

With Ben Lyon

A United Artists Release (November 15, 1930)

CAST

Ben Lyon, James Hall, Jean Harlow, John Darrow, Lucien Prival, Frank Clarke, Roy Wilson, Douglas Gilmore, Jane Winton, Evelyn Hall, William B. Davidson, Wyndham Standing, Carl von Haartman, F. Schumann-Heink, Stephen Carr, Pat Somerset.

CREDITS

Produced and directed by Howard Hughes. Adaptation and Continuity by Howard Estabrook and Harry Behn from a story by Marshall Neilan and Joseph Moncure March. Dialogue by Joseph Moncure March. Photography by Gastano Gaudio, Harry Perry, E. Burton Steene, Elmer Dyer, Zech and Dewey Wrigley. Musical Arrangement by Hugo Riesenfeld. Edited by Frank Lawrence, Douglass Biggs, Perry Hollingsworth.

SYNOPSIS

Two brothers, Monte (Ben Lyon) and Ray Rutledge (James Hall), leave their studies at Oxford to join the British Royal Flying Corps at the outbreak of the first World War. Ray is in love with a girl named Helen (Jean Harlow) who, he believes, returns his affections honestly. When Monte meets Helen and when she readily has an affair with him, Monte realizes that Helen is faithful to no one but herself.

Until the night before he and Monte leave to blow up a

With James Hall

German munitions center, Ray still believes that Helen is his girl.
That night, the two brothers call on Helen and find her in the
arms of another man. Ray realizes he was a fool and has a night
on the town with Monte in order to forget. Although they succeed
in their war mission, Monte and Ray are forced to make a crash
landing. The Germans capture them and offer them safety on
the condition that they reveal the date of the British attack.
Shell-shocked and fearful, Monte runs to give the information,

despite Ray's attempts to stop him. Ray is forced to shoot his brother, but Monte forgives him before he dies. Ray is executed by a German firing squad, but his self-sacrifice has saved the lives of many of his comrades.

This film was Jean's big break. She was on her way up quickly, and in 1931 she appeared in five films.

With James Hall

With Ben Lyon

With Douglas Gilmore and James Hall

What the critics said about

HELL'S ANGELS

Mordaunt Hall
New York Times
  In every instance so soon as the producer forgets Helen, the flaxen-haired creature, and takes to the war, his film is absorbing and exciting. But while she is the centre of attraction the picture is a most mediocre piece of work. . . . Jean Harlow figures as the faithless Helen.

Bland Johaneson
New York Daily Mirror
  It is in the action that *Hell's Angels* packs its punch. . . . The air

shots are awesome, thrilling and impressive; they make the picture
a sensationally exciting one. . . . Lyon, who almost allowed himself
to be forgotten by working three years in this picture, gives a
great account of himself. Jean Harlow, the girl, is fine. A beauty
with plenty of lure. Hall is excellent.

Richard Watts, Jr.
New York Herald Tribune
   The acting will suffice, but that is the best that can be said of it.
Mr. Lyon has most of the opportunities and he does fairly well
and Miss Harlow has at least one realistic scene in which she makes
pretty ardent love to Mr. Lyon.

Thornton Delehanty
New York Post
   Hell's Angels, which had a double opening last night at the
Criterion and Gaiety Theatres, justifies the vast sums of money
which are said to have been spent on it, in the sheer opulence of
its aerial photography. . . . In contrast with its pictorial realism,
the acting of *Hell's Angels* is not so convincing. Even in pantomime
it would be hard to accept Jean Harlow as an English girl
or Ben Lyon and James Hall as Oxford students.

With Douglas Gilmore, James Hall, and Ben Lyon

The Secret Six

With Wallace Beery and John Mack Brown

A Metro-Goldwyn-Mayer Picture (April 25, 1931)

CAST

Wallace Beery, Lewis Stone, John Mack Brown, Jean Harlow, Marjorie Rambeau, Paul Hurst, Clark Gable, Ralph Bellamy, John Miljan, DeWitt Jennings, Murray Kinnell, Fletcher Norton, Louis Natheaux, Frank McGlynn, Theodore von Eltz.

CREDITS

Directed by George Hill. Written by Frances Marion. Photography by Harold Wenstrom. Edited by Blanche Sewell.

SYNOPSIS

During the prohibition era, Scorpio (Wallace Beery), Mizoski (Paul Hurst), and Franks (Ralph Bellamy) start a bootleg liquor business. When their activities spread to the big city, gangster leader Colimo (John Miljan) becomes anxious. Franks and some underlings pay a visit to Colimo's brother at his club.

Franks kills Colimo's brother and places the blame on Scorpio. Scorpio is wounded and, learning that Franks has pulled a doublecross, kills him. Colimo is also disposed of.

Hank (John Mack Brown) and Carl (Clark Gable), two reporters, set out to investigate the gangland killings. When Scorpio sees them hanging around his café he hires Anne (Jean Harlow) as a cashier to interest them in her and keep them away from him. Six leading businessmen, a group of reformers known only as "The Secret Six," ask Hank to get evidence against the gang. He finds the gun which Scorpio used for his killing, but is followed when discovered. Anne learns that he has the murder weapon and catches up with him on a subway train. Her attempt to warn him proves useless since he is murdered.

Angered by the murder, Anne cooperates with the law in bringing Scorpio to trial, but Scorpio is acquitted by a fixed jury and has her kidnapped. Carl learns where Anne is being held but is captured himself when he arrives there. The reformers and the police raid the hideout while Carl gets Anne to safety. Scorpio attempts to flee with Newton (Lewis Stone), his lawyer and the brains of the organization. In an argument over splitting the cash they are carrying, Scorpio shoots Newton who, before he dies, repays Scorpio in kind.

Jean's first film with Gable and Beery. Both Jean and Gable were to become two of Hollywood's biggest stars only a year later.

With John Mack Brown and Clark Gable

With John Mack Brown

With John Mack Brown and Wallace Beery

With Lewis Stone

What the critics said about

THE SECRET SIX

Mordaunt Hall
New York Times

   Jean Harlow, the ash-blonde of several other such tales, once again appears as the girl in the case. . . . The picture moves along swiftly and the dialogue is quite well written.

Bland Johaneson
New York Daily Mirror

   Miss Jean Harlow plays Beery's girl friend, a plausible character softened by love for the reporter. . . . *The Secret Six* is another neat gang melodrama, genuinely thrilling.

Thornton Delehanty
New York Post

   The picture is unusually well directed and it moves with a pulsating speed. . . . The acting, too, is generally on a high level.

The Iron Man

With Lew Ayres

With Lew Ayres and Robert Armstrong

A Universal Picture (April 30, 1931)

CAST
Lew Ayres, Robert Armstrong, Jean Harlow, John Miljan, Eddie Dillon, Mike Donlin, Morrie Cohan, Mary Doran, Mildred Van Dorn, Ned Sparks, Sam Blum.

CREDITS
Directed by Tod Browning. Produced by Carl Laemmle, Jr. Screenplay by Francis Edward Faragoh from the novel by W. R. Burnett. Photography by Percy Hilburn. Edited by Milton Carruth.

SYNOPSIS
Regan (Robert Armstrong) is friend as well as manager to prize fighter Young Mason (Lew Ayres). Mason's big interest in life is his wife Rose (Jean Harlow), but Rose is interested only in money. When Mason loses his opening fight, Rose packs her bags and leaves for Hollywood, hoping to get into films.

With Claire Whitney and John Miljan

With Rose gone, Mason concentrates on prizefighting and is successful. Rose has failed in Hollywood and, seeing that her husband is achieving some measure of fame, she returns to him, much to Regan's displeasure. When Regan voices his disapproval of Rose to Mason, Mason strikes him. In disgust, Regan tears up his contract. Rose then convinces her husband to hire her secret lover, Lewis (John Miljan) as his manager. Lewis, however, manages Mason very badly and consequently Mason is not in condition for a big fight.

Just before the big fight, Regan comes to see Mason. He finds a letter from Lewis' wife, stating that she is naming Rose as correspondent in her divorce suit against Lewis. Mason sees it and throws Rose and Lewis out of his room and out of his life. He loses the big fight but is a wiser man.

This was Jean's only leading role at Universal and her only film with Lew Ayres.

With Mary Doran and Tom Kennedy

What the critics said about

THE IRON MAN

Richard Watts, Jr.
New York Herald Tribune
  . . . *Iron Man* is an earnest and interesting motion picture. . . .
The treacherous wife is played by Miss Jean Harlow, of *Hell's
Angels*, who is not one of this department's favorite actresses.
Even an unfriendly witness must confess, however, that her
artificial qualities fit her present role perfectly and result in a
genuinely effective portrayal.

Andre Sennwald
New York Times
  W. R. Burnett's novel of the prize fighter who loved his wife
too well is at the Globe in a screen transcription that boasts two
exhilarating performances by Lewis Ayres and Robert Armstrong.
. . . It is unfortunate that Jean Harlow, whose virtues as an
actress are limited to her blonde beauty, has to carry a good share
of the picture.

Irene Thirer
New York Daily News
  Ayres' popularity is justified. . . . We wish we could report as
highly on the performance of the platinum blonde, alias Jean
Harlow. Miss Harlow looks stunning in clothes, but she doesn't
exactly get the hang of motion picture histrionics. We mustn't
forget that despite all the Harlow exploitation, the young
woman is practically new to talkies.

With John Miljan

With Lew Ayres

With James Cagney, Leslie Fenton, and Dorothy Gee

The Public Enemy

A Warner Brothers Picture (May 15, 1931)

CAST

James Cagney, Eddie Woods, Jean Harlow, Joan Blondell, Beryl Mercer, Donald Cook, Mae Clarke, Mia Marvin, Leslie Fenton, Robert Emmett O'Connor, Murray Kinnell, Ben Hendricks, Jr., Rita Flynn, Snitz Edwards.

CREDITS

Directed by William A. Wellman. Screenplay by Harvey Thew from a story by Kubec Glasmon and John Bright. Photography by Dev Jennings. Edited by Ed McCormick.

Two friends, Tom Powers (James Cagney) and Matt Doyle (Eddie Woods), start their career of criminal activities with petty thefts and later graduate to big-time rackets. Tom's brother, Mike, (Donald Cook), cannot convince Tom to reform, but manages to keep their mother (Beryl Mercer) from knowing about his activities.

Tom and Matt become involved in bootlegging when prohibition comes in. Tom tires of his mistress Kitty (Mae Clarke) to the extent of pushing a grapefruit in her face at breakfast. He then discovers Gwen Allen (Jean Harlow), and is infatuated with her, although she drives him to the point of desperation by fending off his advances. Gwen begins to respond only when Tom is on the verge of breaking off with her.

When rival gangsters kill Matt, Tom avenges him by machine-gunning the murderers. Tom, however, is wounded and hospitalized. Friends of the men he killed take him from the hospital and murder him, leaving his body at the door of his mother's home.

This was Jean's only lead role at Warner Brothers and her only film with James Cagney.

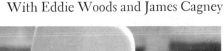

With Eddie Woods and James Cagney

Jean Harlow and James Cagney (in center)

What the critics said about

THE PUBLIC ENEMY

Richard Watts, Jr.
New York Herald Tribune

There is about *The Public Enemy* a quality of grim directness, Zola-esque power and chilling credibility, which makes it far more real and infinitely more impressive than the run of gangster films. . . . It seems to me, however, that Miss Jean Harlow completely ruins the scene in which an attempt is made to show the comparative values of shooting and loving in the animal mind of our amiable hero.

Thornton Delehanty
New York Post

James Cagney contributes one of the best of the screen's many gangster portraits. It is a keen, vivid, and sharply humorous performance. . . . There are some realistic characterizations by Leslie Fenton, Robert Emmett O'Connor, Joan Blondell, Jean Harlow, Murray Kinnell, Ben Hendricks, Jr.

Mordaunt Hall
New York Times

The acting throughout is interesting, with the exception of Jean Harlow, who essays the role of a gangster's mistress.

With Eddie Woods and James Cagney

With Leslie Fenton

With Eddie Kane

Goldie

With Spencer Tracy

A Fox Picture (June 28, 1931)

CAST

Spencer Tracy, Warren Hymer, Jean Harlow, Lina Basquette, Leila Karnelly, Eleanor Hunt, Maria Alba, Ivan Linow, Jesse DeVorska, Eddie Kane.

CREDITS

Directed by Benjamin Stoloff. Written by Gene Towne and Paul Perez. Photography by Ernest Palmer. Edited by Alex Troffey.

SYNOPSIS

Spike (Warren Hymer), second mate on a ship, finds a book of girls' addresses. When he takes the girls out on dates, he finds that each one is tattooed. Spike would like nothing better than to find the man who made these tattoos as a mark of conquest, and to give him a beating. When he finds his adversary in the person of Bill (Spencer Tracy), a sailor, Spike makes a friend of him instead.

In Calais, Spike falls in love with Goldie (Jean Harlow), a high-diver at a carnival. Knowing that the girl is a gold-digger, Bill tries to warn Spike about her, but Spike refuses to listen and even gives Goldie money to keep for him. Goldie tries to win Bill over, but he is not taken in by her machinations.

Spike's eyes are opened when he discovers Bill's tattoo mark on Goldie. He gets his money back and walks out on her, realizing that Bill was trying to protect him.

Goldie was Jean's only lead in a Fox film. It was her first film with Spencer Tracy. The two became a screen team later on at Metro-Goldwyn-Mayer.

With Warren Hymer and Spencer Tracy

With Spencer Tracy

What the critics said about

GOLDIE

Irene Thirer
New York Daily News

By the way, if Caddo Productions, to which firm she is under contract are still looking for a descriptive name for Jean, I would suggest the borrowed blonde, for since her sensational introduction in *Hell's Angels* she has been borrowed by one producing company after another in Hollywood. She is a decorative person but lacks the spark needed to make her shine as a personality.

Bland Johaneson
New York Daily Mirror

Goldie is lively, broad, funny, and a good midsummer movie. . . . Miss Harlow [is] as usual, the platinum blonde Miss Harlow. Tracy and Hymer work splendidly together and make the seafaring rogues immensely likeable.

With Robert Williams

Platinum Blonde

With Robert Williams, Louise Closser Hale,
Reginald Owen, and Donald Dillaway

A Columbia Picture (October 31, 1931)

CAST

Loretta Young, Robert Williams, Jean Harlow, Louise Closser
Hale, Donald Dillaway, Reginald Owen, Walter Catlett,
Edmund Breese, Halliwell Hobbs.

CREDITS

Directed by Frank Capra. Adaptation by Jo Swerling from a
story by Harry E. Chandler and Douglas W. Churchill. Continuity

With Robert Williams

With Halliwell Hobbs, Walter Catlett,
Louise Closser Hale, and Reginald Owen

With Reginald Owen and
Louise Closser Hale

by Dorothy Howell. Dialogue by Robert Riskin. Photography by Joseph Walker. Edited by Gene Milford.

SYNOPSIS

A chorus girl threatens to sue wealthy Michael Schuyler (Donald Dillaway) for breach of promise. Stew Smith (Robert Williams), a newspaper reporter, acquires the incriminating letters Michael wrote to the girl. His concern for the family's good name stems from his interest in Michael's sister Anne (Jean Harlow).

A girl reporter (Loretta Young), known to everyone as Gallagher, loves Smith. Smith, however, marries Anne, the platinum blonde. Shortly after, he tires of his existence as the husband of a socialite. Bored by the snobbishness and sterility around him, he asks Gallagher to come to the Schuyler mansion to help him write a play. Other reporters come with her, and soon the serene mansion is the scene of a merry party.

Anne arrives home and orders everyone to leave. Smith, no longer in love with his wife, leaves with his friends. Smith and Anne agree to a divorce and Smith is now free to prepare for a new life with newsgal Gallagher.

The first of Jean's two lead roles for Columbia. Her co-star, Robert Williams, died shortly after he made this film. Like Jean, he was young and had a promising career ahead of him.

With Robert Williams and
Halliwell Hobbs

With Robert Williams and
Loretta Young

What the critics said about

PLATINUM BLONDE

Richard Watts, Jr.
New York Herald Tribune
   . . . it is a colorful, fast and snappy story for the most part which
awaits you at the Strand, and it is well acted by Robert Williams
in the hero's role. . . . Miss Harlow, as the society girl, is
competent but not much more, while Loretta Young seems
better than usual as the newspaper girl.

Bland Johaneson
New York Daily Mirror
   Can Frank Capra make pictures! From the thriller *Dirigible*
to the moving *Ladies of Leisure*, now the versatile Capra has turned
out one of the gayest, sauciest comedies you've ever seen.
The banal title, *Platinum Blonde*, doesn't even hint at the fun
packed into this riotous picture of an impertinent newspaperman.
. . . Jean Harlow flaunts the famous Harlow figure and acts
effectively the role of the heiress.

Regina Crewe
New York American
   There's lots of fun in the film, and a cracker-jack performance
by Mr. Williams, who carries about eighty percent of the
histrionic burden. For all her top billing, Jean Harlow has very
little to do, and Loretta Young even less. To say they are
competent to the picture's requirements is only a mild compliment.

With Loretta Young

With Walter Byron

Three Wise Girls

With Armand Kaliz

A Columbia Picture (January 11, 1932)

CAST

Jean Harlow, Mae Clarke, Walter Byron, Marie Prevost, Andy Devine, Natalie Moorhead, Jameson Thomas, Lucy Beaumont, Katherine C. Ward, Robert Dudley, Marcia Harris, Walter Miller, Armand Kaliz.

CREDITS

Directed by William Beaudine. Adaptation by Agnes C. Johnson from a story by Wilson Collison. Dialogue by Robert Riskin. Photography by Ted Tetzlaff. Edited by Jack Dennis.

SYNOPSIS

Cassie Barnes (Jean Harlow), a small-town girl, learns that her friend Gladys Kane (Mae Clarke) is doing well in New York, and decides to go there to try her luck. She shares an apartment with a girl named Dot (Marie Prevost). After leaving one job because of an amorous boss, Cassie finds another job as a model where Gladys is employed.

She meets young and wealthy Jerry Dexter (Walter Byron) and they fall in love. Cassie discovers, however, that Dexter is married, and when he tells her that he is asking his wife for a divorce, she refuses to believe him. Gladys has the same problems

With Andy Devine and Walter Byron

with her man, Phelps (Jameson Thomas). Bored with Gladys, Phelps returns to his wife. When Gladys commits suicide, Cassie returns to her home town disillusioned.

Dexter and his wife agree to a divorce and Dexter, with Dot accompanying him, drives to Cassie's home town. When Cassie realizes that Dexter really has been in love with her, she promises to marry him after his divorce becomes final.

After this one for Columbia, Jean's future films would all be for Metro-Goldwyn-Mayer.

With Mae Clarke

Jean Harlow, (Unknown player)

With Walter Byron

What the critics said about

THREE WISE GIRLS

Variety

Jean Harlow has the lead—the girl who keeps straight. She does
her best to suggest the innocent young thing and does better
than might be expected, but she fails to be convincing, and
Mae Clarke takes the acting honors from her.

Motion Picture Herald

Jean Harlow, Marie Prevost and Mae Clark are the three
wise girls who, rather than being wise originally, gain their wisdom
after a few experiences, which have been often recounted in the
song and story of the modern mode.

With Wallace Ford

The Beast of the City

With Wallace Ford

A Metro-Goldwyn-Mayer Picture (February 13, 1932)

CAST

Walter Huston, Jean Harlow, Wallace Ford, Jean Hersholt, Dorothy Peterson, Tully Marshall, John Miljan, Emmett Corrigan, Warner Richmond, Sandy Roth, J. Carrol Naish, Mickey Rooney, Julie Haydon.

CREDITS

Directed by Charles Brabin. Screenplay by John Lee Mahin from a story by W. R. Burnett. Photography by Barney McGill. Edited by Ralph Dawson.

SYNOPSIS

During the prohibition era, police captain Jim Fitzpatrick (Walter Huston) tries to put racketeer Sam Belmonte (Jean Hersholt) behind bars, but his lack of success causes his chief to assign him to a quiet precinct. When Fitzpatrick distinguishes himself by capturing a pair of robbers, a reform commission makes him the new police chief.

As police chief, Fitzpatrick is hindered in his attempts to stop

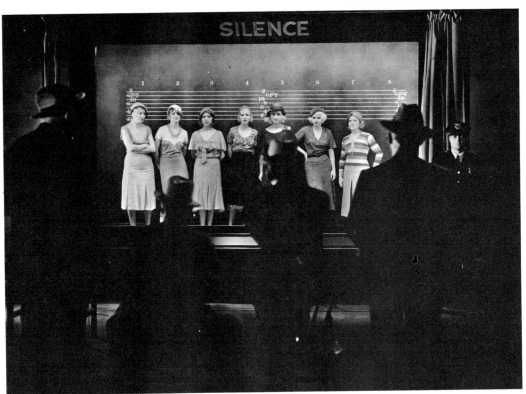

Jean Harlow (sixth from left)

racketeering because he steps on some prominent toes. Fitzpatrick's brother Ed (Wallace Ford) is another thorn in his side because he wants quick promotion in the police department. In addition, Ed is dishonest; asked to keep an eye on Daisy (Jean Harlow) because she was connected with Belmonte, he fell prey to the girl's charms and took payoffs from the gangsters on his beat.

Ed is assigned to guard a shipment of money while it is transported to a bank. He informs Daisy, who persuades him to join Belmonte's gang in stealing the shipment. Police foil the attempted robbery and Ed is indicted with the others. A frightened jury lets the gang off free. Fitzpatrick realizes that he cannot bring Belmonte to justice by legal means, so he and twelve other policemen decide to have a showdown with Belmonte, although they realize they will probably die.

Ashamed of his part in the robbery, Ed joins them. He goes to the nightclub where Belmonte and his gang are celebrating, threatens Belmonte, and is shot down. Fitzpatrick and his twelve friends enter, and a gun battle begins. Police and gangsters die, along with Daisy, who is hit by a bullet as she tries to flee.

With Wallace Ford

What the critics said about

THE BEAST OF THE CITY

Thornton Delehanty
New York Post

It is a well written story, brilliantly directed, and its excitements seem to spring from natural causes rather than any artificialities imposed on them by the author. . . . In addition to Walter Huston's splendid portrayal of the police officer, there are excellent characterizations by Wallace Ford as the weakling brother, Jean Hersholt as the gang leader, Jean Harlow as a gang girl, and Tully Marshall as the aforementioned lawyer.

Irene Thirer
New York Daily News

Enacting the role of a dynamic officer of the law, Walter Huston is invariably at his best. . . . Besides the admirable performance of the star, there is extra special work by Wallace Ford and Jean Harlow. Yep, the platinum blonde baby really acts in this one, mighty well.

Mordaunt Hall
New York Times

In this production, Charles Brabin, the director, wisely heeded the descriptive writing of the author, W. R. Burnett, with the result that the shadow version of the tale is endowed with vitality and realism, the various characters being exceptionally true to life. . . . Jean Harlow, the first of the platinum blondes, is a distinct asset to this film.

With Wallace Ford

With Chester Morris

Red-Headed Woman

With Lewis Stone

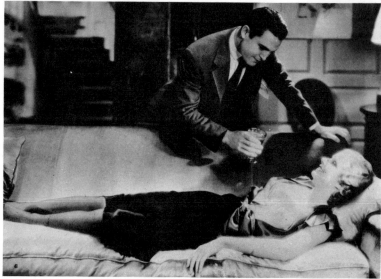

With Chester Morris

A Metro-Goldwyn-Mayer Picture (June 25, 1932)

CAST

Jean Harlow, Chester Morris, Lewis Stone, Leila Hyams, Una Merkel, Henry Stephenson, May Robson, Charles Boyer, Harvey Clark.

CREDITS

Directed by Jack Conway. Screenplay by Anita Loos from the novel by Katharine Brush. Photography by Harold G. Rosson. Edited by Blanche Sewell.

SYNOPSIS

Lil Andrews (Jean Harlow) works for the Legendre Company and works on wealthy Bill Legendre (Chester Morris). Bill becomes so infatuated with Lil that he divorces his wife Irene (Leila Hyams), and marries her.

Although she is now wealthy, Lil is rejected in social circles.

With Chester Morris

To get her way, she forces powerful and wealthy businessman Gaerste (Henry Stephenson) into a compromising situation and compels him to do her bidding. Upon Gaerste's insistence, the socially prominent accept an invitation to a party given by Lil. However, when the guests leave early to go to Irene's home, Lil follows and makes a fool of herself. Later, Bill's father (Lewis Stone) tells Bill that he suspects Lil and Gaerste are intimate. Lil has also been familiar with the chauffeur, Albert (Charles Boyer).

When Lil goes to New York and successfully lures Gaerste into a promise of marriage, her husband informs Gaerste about Lil and Albert. Her big chance gone, Lil tries to reconcile with Bill, and when he refuses, she wounds him with a gunshot. Lil is freed and gets a divorce. Bill remarries Irene and settles down to a sane existence. One day, at the Grand Prix, the Legendres see Lil receive the winner's trophy for a horse she owns. Lil has become the mistress of a titled nobleman. She is living well and retains Albert as her chauffeur.

This film presents Charles Boyer in one of his minor parts before he reached stardom in *Algiers*.

With Chester Morris

With Chester Morris

With Henry Stephenson

What the critics said about

RED-HEADED WOMAN

Lucius Beebe
New York Herald Tribune
   All this viciousness, and a dose of gratuitous snideness to boot, is transferred to the screen version of *Red-Headed Woman*, which was presented to a generously admiring audience yesterday at the Capitol as a fast and at times hilarious satirical comedy. . . . Whether the pleasure of the first audience of the picture was derived from appreciation of Miss Harlow's satirical characterization of a feminine type, or from the belief that she is the hottest number since Helen of Troy started her career of firing topless towers, was difficult to determine. That it enjoyed the film vastly was patent.

Irene Thirer
New York Daily News

    Red-Headed Woman—red hot cinema! The Capitol's current offering is lurid and laugh-enticing in the bigger and better box-office manner. And the ex-platinum Jean Harlow now sparkles as a titian siren, her emoting improved immeasurably along with the change in the shade of her tresses. Svelte, slender and seductive, Harlow gives a splendid performance, making the picture more a character study of a woman who trades on her physical charms than a narrative romance.

Bland Johaneson
New York Daily Mirror

    Filled with laughs and loaded with dynamite, it exposes the males as chumps and convincingly describes what the tired businessman likes. The answer is Harlow. This shapely beauty gives a performance which will amaze you, out-Bowing the famed Bow as an exponent of elemental lure and crude man-baiting technique.

With Leila Hyams and Chester Morris

With Clark Gable

Red Dust

With Forrester Harvey

A Metro-Goldwyn-Mayer Picture (October 22, 1932)

CAST
  Clark Gable, Jean Harlow, Gene Raymond, Mary Astor,
Donald Crisp, Tully Marshall, Forrester Harvey, Willie Fung.

CREDITS
  Produced and directed by Victor Fleming. Screenplay by John
Lee Mahin from the play by Wilson Collison. Photography by
Harold G. Rosson. Edited by Blanche Sewell.

SYNOPSIS
  Dennis Carson (Clark Gable) is in charge of a rubber

With Tully Marshall

plantation in a remote spot in Indo-China, where he and two assistants, McHarg (Tully Marshall) and Guidon (Donald Crisp), oversee the native workers. Returning from Saigon, Guidon arrives on the same boat as Vantine (Jean Harlow), a prostitute on the run from the police. She comes to stay at the plantation's headquarters, where Carson and McHarg find her repulsing a drunken Guidon. Carson is forced to let her stay until the next boat arrives. He is indifferent to her at first, but when he perceives that she is sensitive and kind despite her profession, he succumbs to her charms and presses her to accept money for a stake when her boat arrives.

Gary Willis (Gene Raymond) arrives with his bride Barbara (Mary Astor). An engineer, Willis is prepared to begin work but is stricken with fever. While Carson is nursing Willis back to health, Vantine returns, because the boat has broken down. Carson, however, has begun to fall in love with Barbara and

With Willie Fung
and Gene Raymond

With Clark Gable

With Clark Gable

ignores her. When Willis is well, Carson sends him, along with McHarg and Guidon, to supervise the erection of a bridge in the jungle. During this period Carson and Barbara become involved with one another.

Willis returns and Carson feels ashamed because Willis considers him a great man. He also realizes that Barbara could never share his plantation existence, and in order to make her leave him, he takes up with Vantine and tells Barbara that he is through with her. Barbara becomes furious and wounds Carson with a gunshot. When Willis comes in, Vantine covers up for Barbara and says that Carson had made advances and that Barbara was only protecting herself. Willis quits his job and prepares to leave his wife; Vantine stays to help Carson care for his wound, and Carson decides that she is the woman for him.

This was Jean's second film with Clark Gable, who repeated his role in M-G-M's elaborate remake of *Red Dust*, called *Mogambo*, in 1953. Ava Gardner played the Harlow role and Grace Kelly appeared in Mary Astor's part.

With Mary Astor

With Clark Gable, Gene Raymond,
and Mary Astor

With Clark Gable

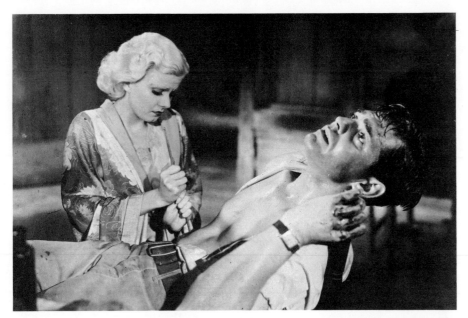

With Clark Gable

What the critics said about

RED DUST

Time Magazine

Given *Red Dust's* brazen moral values, Gable and Harlow have
full play for their curiously similar sort of good-natured toughness.
The best lines go to Harlow. She bathes hilariously in a rain
barrel, reads Gable a bedtime story about a chipmunk and a rabbit.
Her effortless vulgarity, humor, and slovenliness make a noteworthy
characterization, as good in the genre as the late Jeanne Eagels'
Sadie Thompson.

Richard Watts, Jr.
New York Herald Tribune

The flagrantly blonde Miss Harlow, who hitherto has attracted
but intermittent enthusiasm from this captious department,
immediately becomes one of its favorites by her performance in
Red Dust. . . . In the new film she is called upon to go in for
the playing of amiably sardonic comedy and, by managing it with
a shrewd and engagingly humorous skill, she proves herself a
really deft comedienne. . . . You know, too, that these tales are,
as a rule, things to be questioned, if not avoided. Thereupon, to
everyone's surprise—including, possibly, the producers'—Miss
Harlow's comedy, which supplies a running commentary on the
course of the story, came along and transformed *Red Dust* into
an entertaining photoplay. . . . In addition, however, to being
amusing, she manages to create a credible character and to make
the girl she plays a most engaging and sympathetic person.

Hold Your Man

With Clark Gable

With Clark Gable

A Metro-Goldwyn-Mayer Picture (July 7, 1933)

CAST

Jean Harlow, Clark Gable, Stuart Erwin, Dorothy Burgess,
Muriel Kirkland, Garry Owen, Barbara Barondess, Paul Hurst,
Elizabeth Patterson.

CREDITS

Produced and directed by Sam Wood. Screenplay by Anita Loos
and Howard Emmett Rogers from a story by Anita Loos.

With Dorothy Burgess and Clark Gable

Photography by Harold G. Rosson. Edited by Frank Sullivan.

SYNOPSIS

When Eddie Hall (Clark Gable), a confidence man, runs into the apartment of Ruby Adams (Jean Harlow) in order to escape from the police, life becomes complicated for the young girl. She falls in love with the criminal, gives up the idea of marriage with her honest boyfriend Al Simpson (Stuart Erwin), and even waits for Hall, when he is caught and sentenced to a short jail term.

With Clark Gable

With Clark Gable

With Garry Owen and Clark Gable

To make Hall jealous, Ruby tells him that she has been seeing
Mitchell (Paul Hurst), a laundry owner. Hall and his
pal Slim (Garry Owen) cook up a scheme to frame Mitchell
and collect blackmail money. Hall intends to catch Mitchell
making advances at Ruby and, pretending to be her brother,
to agree to accept compensation. However, when Hall sees Ruby
trying to escape from Mitchell's clutches, he becomes genuinely
enraged and knocks Mitchell down. He then grabs Ruby and
takes her to City Hall to get a marriage license. When they return,
they discover that Mitchell has died, having knocked his head
against the wall in the scuffle.

Hall flees and leaves the girl to face the charges. She is sent to

With Paul Hurst, Clark Gable, and Garry Owen

a reformatory, where she discovers that she is going to give birth to Hall's child. Gypsy (Dorothy Burgess), a paroled inmate and once Hall's girl, tells Hall of Ruby's predicament. He comes to the reform school, and he and Ruby are secretly married by a preacher who is there visiting his daughter. Hall is arrested and takes the blame for Mitchell's death. Ruby is released and later gives birth to a boy. After he serves his sentence, Hall joins them to make a fresh start.

This was Jean's third film with Gable.

With Dorothy Burgess

With Clark Gable, Wade Boteler, and Joseph Sawyer

With Stuart Erwin

What the critics said about

HOLD YOUR MAN

Frank S. Nugent
New York Times

Sam Wood's direction is effective and the action is fast, but the sudden transition from hard-boiled, wise-cracking romance to sentimental penitence provides a jolt. Miss Harlow and Mr. Gable will not disappoint their admirers.

Kate Cameron
New York Daily News

Jean Harlow gives a pretty good imitation of a tough baby as Ruby Adams, and she surprises us by showing that she packs a powerful wallop in her delicate-looking left arm. When Dorothy Burgess, as Gypsy, slaps Miss Harlow across the face, the latter returns a short jab with her left hand to Dorothy's chin that look like a stunner. Everybody in the picture, except Stuart Erwin, who plays one of Ruby's suitors, is tough.

Marguerite Tazelaar
New York Herald Tribune

Miss Harlow is good in the beginning, excelling as she does in these hardboiled types, although we regretted to scent a touch of the Mae West technique in her acting, but later, in the subdued poor-caught-creature exhibit, she seemed miscast.

With Clark Gable

With Una Merkel

Bombshell

With Frank Morgan

With Pat O'Brien

A Metro-Goldwyn-Mayer Picture (October 13, 1933)

CAST

Jean Harlow, Lee Tracy, Frank Morgan, Franchot Tone, Pat O'Brien, Una Merkel, Ted Healy, Ivan Lebedeff, Isabel Jewell, Louise Beavers, Leonard Carey, Mary Forbes, C. Aubrey Smith, June Brewster.

CREDITS

Directed by Victor Fleming. Associate Producer, Hunt Stromberg. Screenplay by Jules Furthman and John Lee Mahin from a play by Caroline Francke and Mack Crane. Photoplay by Chester Lyons and Harold G. Rosson. Edited by Margaret Booth.

SYNOPSIS

Film star Lola Burns (Jean Harlow) is weary of her roles as a sexpot and of the attendant publicity. She yearns for a new image

With Frank Morgan and Ted Healy

and becomes engaged to a marquis (Ivan Lebedeff), but Space Hanlon (Lee Tracy), a publicity agent for her studio, breaks the engagement by having the marquis arrested as an illegal alien. Film director Jim Brogan (Pat O'Brien) wants Lola to marry him and to continue her career as well. Lola refuses his proposal and decides to adopt a baby. When adoption officials visit her home, however, her father (Frank Morgan) and brother (Ted Healy) ruin her chances.

With Louise Beavers, Frank Morgan, Leonard Carey, William Newell, and Una Merkel

With Isabel Jewell, Frank Morgan, and Ted Healy

Lola goes to Palm Springs to decide about continuing her film career. There, she meets and falls in love with Gifford Middleton (Franchot Tone), who typifies all that she is looking for in a husband. At last, Lola feels she can belong to a cultured and respectable family. Gifford introduces her to his family, but they behave snobbishly when Lola's father arrives. Angered by the Middletons' stuffiness and disapproval of her career and by their affront to her father, Lola leaves Gifford.

With Isabel Jewell, Ted Healy,
Louise Beavers, Una Merkel,
Frank Morgan, and Lee Tracy

With Frank Morgan

With Frank Morgan and
Una Merkel

When she returns to work at the studio, she spots Gifford and,
with him, what she has taken to be his family (which is actually
a group of actors hired by Hanlon). Hanlon makes Lola see—despite
her anger—that he only wanted to prove to her that she belonged
in movies, and not married to some stuffy bore. Lola comes to
the conclusion that Hanlon really cares for her.

This was Jean's first film with Franchot Tone and Lee Tracy.
It is known to many under the title *Blonde Bombshell*, but it was
originally released at *Bombshell*.

With Franchot Tone

What the critics said about

BOMBSHELL

Mordaunt Hall
New York Times

This farce comedy, which is based on an unproduced play by Caroline Francke and Mack Crane, enjoys itself at Hollywood's expense, and as it spins its slangy but mirthful yarn, it has some unexpected and adroitly conceived turns. . . . Miss Harlow is thoroughly in her element as Lola. For the greater part of the time she is a fiery platinum blonde, but when she hopes to be entrusted with an infant, she, as Lola, assumes a strangely quiet and sympathetic mood.

Richard Watts, Jr.
New York Herald Tribune

For those of us who are enthusiasts for the increasing talents of the distinguished Miss Harlow, *Bombshell* is chiefly important for the fact that it provides the first full-length portrait of this amazing young woman's increasingly impressive acting talent. . . . As a bewildered, hectically-living film star, who combines a love of exhibitionism with a certain wistful desire for home and babies—a part which might easily have been transformed into an orgy of embarrassing sentimentality—Miss Harlow reveals again that gift for an amalgamation of sophisticated sex comedy with curiously honest innocence which is the secret of her individuality. There can be no doubt now that she is a distinguished performer. *Bombshell* is important as another step in Miss Harlow's brilliant career.

With Lee Tracy

Dinner at Eight

With Wallace Beery

A Metro-Goldwyn-Mayer Picture (January 12, 1934)

CAST

Marie Dressler, John Barrymore, Wallace Beery, Jean Harlow,
Lionel Barrymore, Lee Tracy, Edmund Lowe, Billie Burke,
Madge Evans, Jean Hersholt, Karen Morley, Louise Closser Hale,
Phillips Holmes, May Robson, Grant Mitchell.

CREDITS

Directed by George Cukor. Produced by David O. Selznick.
Screenplay by Frances Marion and Herman J. Mankiewicz from
the play by George S. Kaufman and Edna Ferber. Photography by
William Daniels. Edited by Ben Lewis.

With Hilda Vaughn

SYNOPSIS

Millicent Jordan (Billie Burke), the wife of shipping magnate Oliver Jordan (Lionel Barrymore), prepares a dinner in honor of the visiting Lord and Lady Ferncliffe. Oliver's business is failing so he invites Dan Packard (Wallace Beery), a promoter and political aspirant, in the hope that Packard will be able to help him out of his difficulties. No one except his doctor, Wayne Talbot (Edmund Lowe), knows of Oliver's heart trouble. Talbot, a ladies' man, has been having an affair with Packard's brash young wife Kitty (Jean Harlow). He is in love with his own wife (Karen Morley), however, and comes to his senses when she tells him that she has known about his various affairs, yet still loves him.

With Wallace Beery

With Wallace Beery

With Wallace Beery

Kitty is aware that her husband is really behind Jordan's troubles. Packard, in turn, suspects that his wife has been unfaithful. Kitty does not want Packard to interfere with her chance to make friends with the socialite Millicent, and threatens to expose his shady deals and spoil his political chances if he ruins Jordan.

Millicent needs an extra man for dinner and invites Larry Renault (John Barrymore), an unemployed but once famous actor. Millicent's daughter Paula (Madge Evans) is in love with Renault and has been seeing him secretly. When Renault's agent Max Kane (Lee Tracy) brings a producer (Jean Hersholt) to speak with him about a show, Renault demands such a huge sum that the producer leaves. Realizing that his career is at an end, Renault commits suicide in his hotel room. Paula finds him dead but Carlotta Vance (Marie Dressler), who is also staying at the hotel, takes her away from the scene. Thus, Paula does not become involved in the case. Carlotta, a famous actress and once romantically involved with Jordan, is also a guest at the dinner.

Lord and Lady Ferncliffe do not show up and Millicent receives the distressing news that her husband has suffered a heart attack. When Packard arrives with Kitty, he offers to help Oliver in his financial plight—thus appeasing Kitty and making himself look like a big man at the same time. Paula arrives and, heeding Carlotta's advice, hides her grief and takes her place at the dinner table with her fiancé (Phillips Holmes). The dinner is served.

This fine film can be seen over and over without any loss of interest on the viewer's part. Jean's performance is as classic as the film. This marked her second and only other film with Lee Tracy, her first with Lionel Barrymore, and her second with Wallace Beery.

With Wallace Beery

With Billie Burke and Wallace Beery

Jean Hersholt, John Barrymore, and Lee Tracy

What the critics said about

DINNER AT EIGHT

Richard Watts, Jr.
New York Herald Tribune

Of them all I think that the amazing Miss Jean Harlow gives the grandest show . . . it seems to me that Miss Harlow, an increasingly delightful actress with each picture, plays the guttersnipe of a wife, who battles with Mr. Beery, her vulgar husband, and makes love to Edmund Lowe, her amorous doctor, with such high spirits, comic gayety, and shrewd knowledge—or perhaps instinct—that among a congress of stars doing their best she is quite the hit of the evening. Of course, it is true that the scenes of marital invective between Miss Harlow and Mr. Beery

Marie Dressler and Madge Evans

are the most entertaining in the play, and *Dinner at Eight*, despite the cinema doctoring, remains chiefly interesting for its component parts. But that does not entirely explain the Harlow triumph.

Mordaunt Hall
New York Times

Mr. Beery fits into the role of Dan Packard as though it were written especially for him and Miss Harlow makes the most of the part of Kitty. It was a grand evening of entertainment.

Bland Johaneson
New York Daily Mirror

A glance at the cast will assure you that the acting of *Dinner at Eight* is wholly splendid. Among all these great performers it is little Jean Harlow who stands out in the role of the coarse and scheming little wife of Wallace Beery. Harlow is magnificent. You'll cheer her performance and heartily applaud every other player in *Dinner at Eight*. It's a great picture. You can't afford to miss it.

With Clara Blandick and Patsy Kelly

The Girl from Missouri

With Lewis Stone and Russell Hopton

With Lionel Barrymore

A Metro-Goldwyn-Mayer Picture (August 3, 1934)

CAST

Jean Harlow, Lionel Barrymore, Franchot Tone, Lewis Stone, Patsy Kelly, Alan Mowbray, Clara Blandick, Hale Hamilton, Henry Kolker, Nat Pendleton.

CREDITS

Directed by Jack Conway. Produced by Bernard H. Hyman. Written by Anita Loos and John Emerson. Photography by Ray June. Music by Dr. William Axt. Edited by Tom Held.

SYNOPSIS

Eadie (Jean Harlow), disgusted with her loose-living parents, goes to New York with her friend, Kitty (Patsy Kelly). Eadie becomes a chorus girl, but her ambition in life is to marry a millionaire. She determines to remain virtuous until the right rich man comes along and marries her. Eadie and a group of chorus girls are sent to entertain at a strictly male party given by Frank Cousins (Lewis Stone). Cousins is despondent because he is broke and hopes Paige (Lionel Barrymore), a millionaire, will

With Lionel Barrymore
and Franchot Tone

With Franchot Tone

With Franchot Tone

lend him money. Paige refuses. Cousins meets Eadie and,
impressed by her freshness and idealism, he presents her with
his gold cuff links. Once alone, Cousins commits suicide. Police
arrive and attempt to arrest Eadie, believing that she has stolen
the cuff links, but Paige supports her statement that they were
a gift.

Eadie decides that Paige is the millionaire for her to marry. She
pursues the widower to his yacht in Florida, where she discovers
his son Tom (Franchot Tone). She falls in love with Tom, and
when he asks her to become his mistress she agrees, in tears.
Tom realizes she was telling the truth about her virtue, although
she is prepared to sacrifice it for love of him. He proposes
marriage, and Eadie happily accepts.

Furious about the matter, Paige frames Eadie by hiring a man

With Alan Mowbray and Lionel Barrymore

to come to her hotel room. When Eadie is arrested, Tom does not believe that she is innocent. Wealthy Charles Turner (Hale Hamilton) pays her bail and she agrees to become his mistress. First, however, she sets out to take revenge on Paige, who is leaving for Europe to attend a peace conference. While he is speaking with reporters, Eadie, clad only in a slip, rushes up to him, hugs him, and retreats. Looking for Eadie because he wants to apologize to her, Tom learns of her actions from his father and realizes that she did it only for revenge. Paige admits he framed Eadie and joins his son in his search for her. They find the girl at Turner's apartment, drunk but still virtuous. Tom marries Eadie in a quick ceremony and Paige explains to reporters that Eadie is his daughter-in-law and was merely demonstrating her filial affection for him. Tom and Eadie look forward to happiness together.

This was Jean's second film with Franchot Tone and Lionel Barrymore.

With Franchot Tone and
Lionel Barrymore

With Franchot Tone

What the critics said about

THE GIRL FROM MISSOURI

Andre Sennwald
New York Times

Miss Harlow, who simply must be accepted as a fine comedienne in her particular sphere, plays her laughs too shrewdly to warrant the frequently heard opinion that not all of her humor is intentional. *The Girl From Missouri* is studded with explosive comedy twists, and the dialogue has much to recommend it.

Richard Watts, Jr.
New York Herald Tribune

Miss Harlow's grim determination to battle for her virtue to the death has, you see, a certain comic spirit to it, rather than the lyric note that probably is demanded in such cases. Yet this increasingly astonishing young actress plays her role with such engaging freshness that it is no wonder that even the New York censors gleefully passed the work celebrating her exploits.

Photoplay Magazine

Noisily defiant, rip-snorting and raucous in spots is this hilarious Jean Harlow opus. Though the lines play pretty safe, it is fast and furious adult fare. Jean is a gorgeous eyeful, with all the right answers—one of those "good girl" chorines out for matrimony and millions, but the two must go together. . . . The scene on the yacht, which Jean visits (uninvited) is a classic in its line.

With Franchot Tone

With Carl Randall

Jean Harlow (in center)

A Metro-Goldwyn-Mayer Picture (April 19, 1935)

CAST

Jean Harlow, William Powell, Franchot Tone, May Robson, Ted Healy, Nat Pendleton, Robert Light, Rosalind Russell, Henry Stephenson, Mickey Rooney, Louise Henry, James Ellison, Leon Waycoff, Man Mountain Dean, Farina, Allan Jones, Carl Randall, and Nina Mae McKinney.

With Mae Robson, Franchot Tone, and William Powell

With Franchot Tone

With William Powell and Rosalind Russell

CREDITS

Directed by Victor Fleming. Produced by David O. Selznick. Screenplay by P. J. Wolfson from a story by Oliver Jeffries. Photography by George Folsey. Edited by Margaret Booth.

SYNOPSIS

Wealthy Bob Harrison (Franchot Tone) buys all the seats in a Broadway theatre for one night just so that he can see a musical starring Mona Leslie (Jean Harlow) all by himself. After the performance, he courts Mona, much to the displeasure of her agent, Ned Riley (William Powell), who has been in love with Mona although he has never let her know it.

Bob jilts his fiancée, Josephine Mercer (Rosalind Russell), and marries Mona. Bob's father (Henry Stephenson) dislikes Mona but Josephine surprisingly makes friends with her. Josephine marries someone else and, at her wedding party, Bob, in a drunken state, tells Josephine that Mona lured him into marriage. Mona hears this and puts on a dance act for the guests in order to hide her grief. Words are exchanged, Bob hits his father and Ned hits Bob.

With (Unknown player) and William Powell

With William Powell

Later, while Ned is discussing Mona's troubles with her, Bob arrives and tries to start a commotion. Ned and Mona put him to bed to sleep it off. Once he is alone, Bob commits suicide. Ned and Mona unjustly become the center of a scandal. When Mona gives birth to Bob's child, her father-in-law tries to take it from her, but she relinquishes her inheritance from Bob in order to keep the child. Ned puts together a show for Mona to star in. On opening night, when the audience shouts insults at her, Mona delivers an honest and straightforward rebuttal to all the false gossip about her and is then cheered by the audience, Bob's father included. Mona gives a fine performance while Ned, backstage, happily plans marriage with her.

Jean's third film with Franchot Tone and her first with William Powell.

What the critics said about

RECKLESS

With William Powell

Richard Watts, Jr.
New York Herald Tribune

The story, supposed to be based on a recent celebrated case, is hardly among the classics of the season, but it does possess a certain unashamed melodramatic effectiveness, thanks in great part to the sincere, straightforward, and generally alluring performance that Miss Harlow brings to it.

Bland Johaneson
New York Daily Mirror

An unbeatable company appears in this melodrama with music. Headed by the great Harlow, William Powell, Franchot Tone, and May Robson, it includes an impressive assembly of Hollywood's most popular actors. . . . *Reckless* is good popular entertainment and the Harlow fans will applaud it enthusiastically.

Regina Crewe
New York American

The show belongs to Miss Harlow, who, with lines and situations tossed like flowers at her feet, acquits herself right nobly, even when she is presumed to sing.

With William Powell

With Wallace Beery and Clark Gable

China Seas

Wallace Beery, Jean Harlow, and others

A Metro-Goldwyn-Mayer Picture (August 16, 1935)

CAST

  Clark Gable, Jean Harlow, Wallace Beery, Lewis Stone,
Rosalind Russell, Dudley Digges, C. Aubrey Smith, Robert
Benchley, William Henry, Live Demaigret, Lillian Bond, Edward
Brophy, Donald Meek, Carol Ann Beery, Akim Tamiroff.

CREDITS

  Directed by Tay Garnett. Associate Producer, Albert Lewin.
Screenplay by Jules Furthman and James Keven McGuinness
from the novel by Crosbie Garstin. Photography by Ray June.
Music by Herbert Stothart. Edited by William Levanway.

SYNOPSIS

  Alan Gaskell (Clark Gable) is captain of a ship that sails on
the China Seas. His ship is scheduled to carry a gold shipment
from Hong Kong to Singapore. Gaskell is fearful of a pirate attack,
since he has already captured some pirates trying to board the ship.
To add to his troubles, China Doll (Jean Harlow), his discarded
mistress, decides to make the trip to Singapore.

With Clark Gable, Rosalind Russell, and C. Aubrey Smith

On board, Gaskell discovers Sybil Barclay (Rosalind Russell), his old English sweetheart. She had married another man but is now a widow and is taking a trip around the world. Once out at sea, Gaskell and Sybil begin to fall in love again. China Doll, desperately in love with Gaskell, makes a fool of herself at the dinner table by implying her relationship with Gaskell. Gaskell tells China Doll that he is through with her and, to console herself, she plays cards and gets drunk with Jamesy Macardle

With Wallace Beery

With Clark Gable

Wallace Beery), a trader who is in love with her. Macardle is
secretly in league with the pirates. When China Doll wins money
from him in the card game, she notices that one of the bills
has Chinese writing on it. Knowing that pirates use this as an
identification piece, she goes to inform Gaskell, but he doesn't
even give her a chance to speak with him.

Angered, China Doll agrees to work with Macardle and steals
the keys to the ship's storeroom for him. When pirates attack
the ship, they learn that Gaskell has moved the gold elsewhere.
Davids (Lewis Stone), a third officer who once was branded a
coward, deliberately falls into the pirate junk with a bag of
grenades—killing the robbers and sacrificing his life in the
explosion. Macardle takes poison, preferring death to imprisonment.

When the ship docks, China Doll is taken into custody for her
part in the raid. Sybil tells Gaskell that he would be happier as
a captain on the China Seas and with China Doll. Gaskell
realizes Sybil is right; he tells China Doll that he will help her
at her trial as well as marry her.

China Seas was Jean's fourth film with Gable and her third—and
last—with Wallace Beery.

What the critics said about

CHINA SEAS

Andre Sennwald
New York Times

In its quieter moments *China Seas* takes the customers into the passenger salon to watch Jean Harlow giving her aloof English rival an amusing lesson in high society deportment. . . . Miss Harlow's exit after the captain refuses to listen to her will have to go on record as one of the season's major examples of etiquette.

Richard Watts, Jr.
New York Herald Tribune

It is my guess you will find all three of the stars conducting themslves more than worthily. Miss Harlow makes the tropical trollop gay and courageous and loyal, which is no small feat, because in less capable hands the girl might have seemed an unpleasantly vindictive virago. But that curious combination of wisdom and innocence that emerges in Miss Harlow's characterization always succeeds in making her a gallant and courageously pathetic figure.

Regina Crewe
New York American

As for the principals, none of the three has ever been better. Miss Harlow, in particular, is at her best, while both Messrs. Gable and Beery add to their already weighty laurels.

With Wallace Beery

With Wallace Beery and Clark Gable

With Wallace Beery

With Spencer Tracy

Riffraff

A Metro-Goldwyn-Mayer Picture (January 3, 1936)

CAST

Jean Harlow, Spencer Tracy, Una Merkel, Joseph Calleia, Victor Kilian, Mickey Rooney, J. Farrell MacDonald, Roger Imhoff, Juanita Quigley, Paul Hurst, Vince Barnett, Dorothy Appleby, Judith Wood, Arthur Housman, Wade Boteler.

CREDITS

Directed by J. Walter Ruben. Associate Producer, David Lewis. Screenplay by Frances Marion from a story by Frances Marion,

With Spencer Tracy

H. W. Hanemann and Anita Loos. Photography by Ray June.
Music by Edward Ward. Edited by Frank Sullivan.

SYNOPSIS

Hattie (Jean Harlow) and her sister Lil (Una Merkel), daughters
of a fisherman (Roger Imhoff), work in a cannery on the
waterfront. Hattie loves Dutch Miller (Spencer Tracy), a tough
and popular fisherman, but Dutch does not pay any attention
to her. At a dance, Nick Appopolis (Joseph Calleia), Hattie's
boss and an unsuccessful suitor, starts an argument with Dutch
for holding Hattie too close during a dance. A fight breaks out,
which Dutch and Hattie flee. Dutch begins to see more of Hattie
and eventually they get married.

It is to Nick's advantage that the fishermen go on strike, so
he hires Red Belcher (Paul Hurst), a professional strike-maker,
to influence Dutch to lead the fishermen on this path. Hattie's
pleas do not swerve Dutch, and he succeeds in calling a strike.
The fishermen suffer because of it and they throw Dutch out
of the union. Dutch breaks up with Hattie and leaves the waterfront.

With Roger Imhoff and Mickey Rooney

When Hattie learns that Dutch is ill and needs money, she asks Nick for it. He refuses, so she steals it from him and goes to Dutch. Dutch refuses her aid, so she gives the money to Belcher to turn over to Dutch later—which Belcher never does. Hattie is sent to prison for the theft and is visited there by Dutch, who has beaten and left Belcher after finding out about Hattie. He wants to help her escape, but she refuses. Hattie has given birth to Dutch's child while in prison. Lil is caring for the child, but Hattie tells Dutch nothing about its birth. She makes Dutch promise to go straight and to wait for her to get out of prison

With Spencer Tracy and
William Newell

With William Newell, Una Merkel,
Roger Imhoff, and Spencer Tracy

With Spencer Tracy and
J. Farrell MacDonald

legally. Dutch returns to the waterfront, but the only job he can get is as a watchman. One night, he stops Belcher from sabotaging one of Nick's ships and this reconciles him with Nick, and soon with the other men as well. Dutch is again free to become a union fisherman. Hattie, mistakenly thinking that Dutch was badly hurt while stopping Belcher, flees prison to meet her husband. When she sees that he is well, she determines to return to prison to serve out her sentence, and tells Dutch that they have a child. They plan a new life together when she is released.

Riffraff was Jean's second film with Spencer Tracy.

With Joseph Calleia

With Una Merkel

What the critics said about

RIFFRAFF

Rose Pelswick
New York Journal
   There's plenty of action in the film, and Miss Harlow and
Mr. Tracy hurl hard-boiled dialogue at each other vigorously.
It's interesting entertainment, dotted with laughs.

Richard Watts, Jr.
New York Herald Tribune
   Miss Harlow not only looks entrancingly handsome, but plays

With Una Merkel

the role of the girl, who for some reason not clear to me, loves the bully of the fishing fleet with her customary straightforward candor.

Bland Johaneson
New York Daily Mirror
    Lively, daring, meaty, and rough, it is the best film Jean Harlow has made for a long time, and she gives a rich performance as the unhappy belle of the fish cannery.

With George Givot and Joseph Calleia

With Myrna Loy and Clark Gable

Wife vs. Secretary

With Clark Gable, May Robson, and Myrna Loy

A Metro-Goldwyn-Mayer Picture (February 28, 1936)

CAST

Clark Gable, Jean Harlow, Myrna Loy, May Robson, George Barbier, James Stewart, Hobart Cavanaugh, Gilbert Emery, Margaret Irving, William Newell, Marjorie Gateson, Gloria Holden, Tom Dugan.

CREDITS

Directed by Clarence Brown. Produced by Hunt Stromberg. Screenplay by Norman Krasna, Alice Duer Miller, John Lee Mahin from a story by Faith Baldwin. Photography by Ray June. Music by Herbert Stothart and Edward Ward. Edited by Frank E. Hull.

SYNOPSIS

Whitey Wilson (Jean Harlow) is secretary to magazine publisher Van Sanford (Clark Gable). Sanford is happily married to Linda (Myrna Loy), and Linda is not envious of the attractive Whitey because she knows her husband regards Whitey only as his secretary. Van's mother (May Robson), however, plants the first seed of suspicion in Linda's mind.

Whitey has her own troubles with boy friend Dave (James

Stewart). They argue and stop seeing each other when Whitey refuses to leave her job to marry him. When Linda requests that Sanford promote Whitey to a higher position, he refuses, stating that she is most valuable to his organization as his secretary.

When Sanford goes to Cuba to close a business deal, Whitey calls him with some important information concerning the transaction. Sanford has her take a plane to Cuba and, with her help, closes the deal; after, they have an innocent celebration. Linda, unaware that Whitey is with her husband, telephones Sanford at his hotel. When Whitey answers his phone, Linda is certain that Sanford and Whitey are having an affair. She leaves Sanford despite his pleas.

Linda intends to take a trip to Europe, but Whitey comes to see her before she leaves. She tells Linda that there has never been anything between herself and Sanford, but that Sanford might take an interest in her when his wife has gone. Linda realizes that she has been a fool and reconciles with Sanford. Whitey reconciles with Dave, now realizing that marriage is more important than her career.

This was Jean's fifth film with Gable.

With Clark Gable

With Myrna Loy

With John Qualen

With Niles Welch and Clark Gable

What the critics said about

WIFE VS. SECRETARY

Frank S. Nugent
New York Times

You may rail, critically, at the glossy stereotype, and you may accuse Miss Baldwin of growing duller and duller in her treatment of her pet plot; but you will realize—with a sense of complete futility—that any Faith Baldwin *Wife vs. Secretary* picture with Gable, Harlow, and Loy is predestined for success. . . . Like most of these Metro super-specials, the film has been richly produced, directed competently by Clarence Brown, and is well-played—within the handicaps of their roles—by Miss Harlow, Myrna Loy, and Mr. Gable.

New York Herald Tribune
Richard Watts, Jr.

The one joy of the film is Miss Harlow. Once more she gets no chance to demonstrate her talents as one of the distinguished comediennes of our time, but always she is so straightforward and human and pleasant to observe that she is of inordinate value to a film that certainly does require her gifts.

With Clark Gable

With James Stewart

With Cary Grant and Franchot Tone

Suzy

With Franchot Tone

With Tyler Brook and Cary Grant

A Metro-Goldwyn-Mayer Picture (June 26, 1936)

CAST

Jean Harlow, Franchot Tone, Cary Grant, Lewis Stone,
Benita Hume, Reginald Mason, Inez Courtney, Greta Meyer,
David Clyde, Tyler Brook, Robert Livingston, Stanley Morner,
Christian Rub, George Spelvin, Una O'Connor.

CREDITS

Directed by George Fitzmaurice. Produced by Maurice Revnes.
Screenplay by Dorothy Parker, Alan Campbell, Horace Jackson,
Lenore Coffee from the novel by Herbert Gorman. Photography
by Ray June. Music by Dr. William Axt. Edited by George Boemler.

SYNOPSIS

Suzy (Jean Harlow) is an American showgirl in London in 1914.
She loves Terry Moore (Franchot Tone), an Irish inventor
working for a London engineering firm owned by a German woman,
Mrs. Schmidt (Greta Meyer).

Terry takes Suzy to the factory on their wedding night to show
her his new invention. Suzy spots Madame Eyrelle (Benita Hume),
an adventuress-spy, going into a meeting with Mrs. Schmidt.
Later, Mrs. Schmidt spots Terry alone and, believing Terry knows
that she heads a German spy ring, she sends Madame Eyrelle
to follow him. Terry brings Suzy to his apartment. Madame
Eyrelle enters with her face covered and shoots Terry.

When Madame Eyrelle flees, Suzy runs away too, fearing she

With Cary Grant and George Davis

will be blamed for Terry's death. Suzy goes to Paris where a friend named Maisie (Inez Courtney) gets her a job in a cabaret. Suzy is unaware that Terry is alive and recovered and that Mrs. Schmidt and her cohorts—except for Madame Eyrelle—have been arrested.

War breaks out, and Suzy meets André Charville (Cary Grant), a famous French aviator. After a whirlwind courtship, Suzy and André get married. André's wealthy father (Lewis Stone) disapproves of the marriage at first, but grows to like his daughter-in-law because she remains loyal to André even though he begins seeing other women.

Terry comes to Paris to have his new plane tested by André. André, however, has been wounded and is in the hospital. When Terry comes to visit him, he meets Suzy. She tries to explain that she fled London thinking him dead but he does not believe

With Inez Courtney

With Cary Grant and Inez Courtney

her. He calls her a gold-digger, but tells no one about their marriage.

Suzy is unaware that Madame Eyrelle is in Paris and seeing André, but one day, she sees a magazine photo of André with the adventuress-spy. She tells Terry that she believes it was Madame Eyrelle who shot him in London. André, scheduled to go on a flying mission, has gone to see this woman at her chateau. Suzy and Terry follow to warn Andre, but the adventuress' henchman shoots and kills him and flees in a car with his chief.

Terry takes André's plane and pursues the car. He machine-guns the auto, which bursts into flames, killing the two passengers. In an encounter with German planes, Terry succeeds in bringing

With Cary Grant

down three of them, after which he cracks up the plane by the chateau.

Suzy tells him that Andre is dead, and they decide to let André's name go unsullied. They place him in the pilot's seat, leading the military to believe that André died as a result of a wound inflicted during the encounter with the enemy planes. André is honored as a hero who died fighting. Terry now believes Suzy is sincere and they start a new life together.

Suzy was Jean's only film with Cary Grant and her fourth, and last, with Franchot Tone.

With Cary Grant

With Lewis Stone

What the critics said about

SUZY

Bland Johaneson
New York Daily Mirror

Miss Harlow looks ravishing, sings pleasantly and acts vigorously. She is a bewitching and lovable Suzy. However bizarre her difficulties, her performance makes them convincing and entertaining.

With Cary Grant

With Cary Grant and Franchot Tone

Richard Watts, Jr.
New York Herald Tribune

I will go on screaming in my customary wilderness that it is a great shame to waste Miss Harlow in such a role, when she should be exercising her vast gifts as a half-sophisticated, half-innocent comic. Nevertheless, she plays her role with her customary honest simplicity.

Irene Thirer
New York Post

The laughs fall to Cary Grant and Franchot Tone, who take turns at being Harlow's cinematic husband. Jean plays practically straight—and she oughtn't to. She's a swell comedienne, and not too adept at drama—especially tragedy.

With Myrna Loy, William Powell, and Spencer Tracy

Libeled Lady

With Spencer Tracy

A Metro-Goldwyn-Mayer Picture (October 9, 1936)

CAST

Jean Harlow, William Powell, Myrna Loy, Spencer Tracy, Walter Connolly, Charley Grapewin, Cora Witherspoon, E. E. Clive, Lauri Beatty, Otto Yamaoka, Charles Trowbridge, Spencer Charters, George Chandler, William Benedict.

CREDITS

Directed by Jack Conway. Produced by Lawrence Weingarten. Screenplay by Maurice Watkins, Howard Emmett Rogers, George Oppenheimer from a story by Wallace Sullivan. Photography by Norbert Brodine. Music by Dr. William Axt. Edited by Frederick Y. Smith.

SYNOPSIS

Warren Haggerty (Spencer Tracy), managing editor of a newspaper, prints a story that wealthy Connie Allenbury (Myrna Loy) tried to steal another woman's husband. The story is false, but Haggerty is unable to retrieve all the copies that went out. Connie gets one and notifies him that she is suing for five million dollars. Haggerty postpones his wedding to Gladys Benton (Jean Harlow), making Gladys furious.

Haggerty hits upon a plan. He hires Bill Chandler (William Powell), who formerly worked for Haggerty but now dislikes him. He persuades Gladys to marry Chandler, although it is to be a marriage in name only. Chandler is to try to get Connie Allenbury to fall in love with him so that, when this is accomplished, Gladys can sue Connie for alienation of Chandler's affections and make Connie's libel suit against the paper meaningless.

Chandler boards the ship on which Connie and her father (Walter Connolly) are returning from England to America. He reads up on fishing to impress Allenbury, who loves the sport. Connie, however, considers Chandler an opportunist and resents him. Arriving in the United States, Allenbury invites Chandler to his estate in the Adirondacks for some fishing. When, by accident, Chandler snags an elusive trout that Allenbury has long been trying to catch, Connie becomes friendlier. Chandler's plan backfires when he and Connie discover that they are really in love with one another. He tries to talk Connie out of the libel suit before he is exposed, but when Haggerty learns that Chandler is serious about Connie, he tells Gladys to go ahead with her alienation suit. Chandler, however, charms Gladys out of it.

When Connie learns from an acquaintace that Chandler is married, she tests Chandler by asking him to marry her. He accepts and a justice of the peace performs the ceremony. When Gladys and Haggerty find out, they come to Chandler's hotel room.

With Spencer Tracy

With Spencer Tracy

With William Powell and Spencer Tracy

Connie tells Haggerty that she has dropped the suit against the paper and Haggerty is satisfied. Gladys, however, is angry at Chandler for charming her and then marrying Connie. Chandler tells her that the divorce she obtained from her first husband in Yucatan by mail was not legal and therefore neither was her marriage to him. Gladys explains that she got a legal divorce in Reno before marrying him. Chandler deliberately punches Haggerty to get Haggerty sympathy from Gladys. The scheme works and Gladys agrees to divorce Chandler and marry Haggerty. Having heard the whole story from Chandler beforehand, Connie is quite happy that she can marry him legally. Her father walks in and is confused by the whole thing.

This was Jean's third film with Tracy and her second with Powell, and it was her last with both.

With Spencer Tracy and William Powell

What the critics said about

LIBELED LADY

Leo Mishkin
New York Telegraph
   The stars of the piece do their work in noble style. Miss Harlow, Heaven be praised, is again a luminous comedienne.

Howard Barnes
New York Herald Tribune
   Miss Harlow, as the tough fiancé of a newspaper editor, who is persuaded into marrying a blackmail artist in order to fight a libel suit, has a part cut to her talents. Her insulting cracks at the editor are gems of brash comedy and she vitalizes the material throughout. She proves anew that she is a really fine comedienne.

Frank S. Nugent
New York Times
   Most of the situations are rousingly funny, particularly Mr. Powell's trout-fishing adventures and the Harlow-Powell marriage scene, in which the bride accepts a peck on the cheek from her husband and throws herself ardently into Mr. Tracy's arms. "A good friend," explains the groom to the minister. "A very good friend," he adds, after a second look. Moments like these impel us to condone a certain slackening of pace toward the picture's conclusion, and we are so pathetically grateful to Metro for restoring Miss Harlow to her proper metier that we could have forgiven even more serious lapses.

With E. E. Clive and William Powell

With Robert Taylor

Personal Property

With Reginald Owen and Robert Taylor

A Metro-Goldwyn-Mayer Picture (March 19, 1937)

CAST
Jean Harlow, Robert Taylor, Reginald Owen, Una O'Connor, Henrietta Crosman, E. E. Clive, Cora Witherspoon, Marla Shelton, Forrester Harvey.

CREDITS
Directed by W. S. Van Dyke II. Produced by John W. Considine, Jr. Screenplay by Hugh Mills and Ernest Vajda from the play Man in Possession by H. M. Harwood. Photography by William Daniels. Music by Franz Waxman. Edited by Ben Lewis.

SYNOPSIS
In England, Robert Dabney (Robert Taylor) returns to his family after serving a jail term for selling a car he did not own. His father (E. E. Clive) and brother Claude (Reginald Owen) consider him irresponsible and would rather not have him around.

The sheriff gives Robert a job and assigns him to watch the house and furniture of a widow, Crystal Wetherby (Jean Harlow),

With Robert Taylor

With Robert Taylor

to make sure that she moves nothing out, since her property has been attached to pay her debts.

Crystal hopes to marry Claude Dabney, believing he is wealthy. The Dabney family is also in financial straits, however, and Claude wants to marry Crystal for the money he thinks she has. Knowing the truth in both cases, Robert finds the whole matter amusing. He even offers to act as butler at a party that Crystal is giving for the Dabney family and some friends. When Claude sees Robert working there, he insists that Crystal fire him, but she refuses.

Claude later gives Robert money to go away and prepares to marry Crystal. On the wedding day, the sheriff's men arrive and start taking away Crystal's furniture. Claude learns that she is broke and then quickly cancels the wedding. Robert knows that Crystal loves him and that only Claude kept them apart. Now with a free field, Robert and Crystal leave on the furniture truck with marriage on their minds.

Personal Property was the only film Jean made with Robert Taylor.

With Robert Taylor

With Marla Shelton, Robert Taylor, and E. E. Clive

What the critics said about

PERSONAL PROPERTY

Bosley Crowther
New York Times

If they will only be patient, all the girls on the M-G-M lot eventually are going to have a twirl at him, it seems. This week it is Jean Harlow who loves Robert Taylor at the Capitol, and th gilded welkin of that de luxe establishment is ringing with feminine coos and delighted soprano laughter. For Mr. Taylor

With Una O'Connor

With Robert Taylor

eing a card is just as irresistible as Mr. Taylor being deadly
erious, with those large Nebraska eyes, whereas, Miss Harlow—
weeping or flouncing through expensive sets in that eternal
egligee of hers—is positively the indignant lady of a Peter Arno
rawing.

rene Thirer
New York Post
This new offering is just as flip and amusing as was its
redecessor. Miss Harlow is at home as the golden-haired gold-
igger with a heart of gold.

Regina Crewe
New York American
Both Mr. Taylor and Miss Harlow have enjoyed roles better
uited to their talent, but Bob plays sincerely and his performance
s both persuasive and convincing. Jean jumps right into character
nd gets everything out of it that was ever written in.

Saratoga

With Clark Gable

With Hattie McDaniels

A Metro-Goldwyn-Mayer Picture (July 23, 1937)

CAST

Clark Gable, Jean Harlow, Lionel Barrymore, Frank Morgan, Walter Pidgeon, Una Merkel, Cliff Edwards, George Zucco, Jonathan Hale, Hattie McDaniels, Frankie Darro, Henry Stone.

CREDITS

Directed by Jack Conway. Produced by Bernard H. Hyman. Written by Anita Loos and Robert Hopkins. Photographed by Ray June. Music by Edward Ward. Edited by Elmo Vernon.

SYNOPSIS

Carol Layton (Jean Harlow) returns to the United States after a stay in England. She has become engaged to wealthy Hartley Madison (Walter Pidgeon), an American businessman. Her father (Jonathan Hale), a horse breeder at Saratoga, owes bookie Duke Bradley (Clark Gable) a huge amount of money as a result of gambling losses, and gives him the deed to his breeding farm to cancel the debt. He does this because he realizes he is seriously ill and wants no debts left behind.

Carol takes an immediate dislike to Bradley when she meets him, but he is attracted to her. When Layton dies of a heart attack at the race track, Carol and her grandfather (Lionel Barrymore) discover that they are broke. Bradley wants to give the deed back to Carol without payment, but she refuses—hoping Madison will give her the money to pay Bradley. Carol sells the last horse she

With Walter Pidgeon

owns at an auction. Madison buys it and Carol uses the money to place bets on horse races with Bradley. She wins a great deal of money from Bradley, but discovers she is in love with him.

Bradley lures Madison back to Saratoga by telling him Carol is ill. He hopes to get Madison to place bets with him and thereby to win back all the money he lost to Carol. When Carol tells Bradle she loves him, he lets her in on his plans.

When Bradley gets Madison to place a big bet on a horse with him, however, Carol deliberately hires a tough and unscrupulous jockey to ride. Although Bradley learns this, he refuses to welch on the deal. Carol, seeing him prefer to lose everything rather than go back on his word, realizes that he is basically honest. She makes her mind up then and there that she will marry him.

The race turns out to be a surprise for everyone because Madison horse loses. Bradley tells Carol he loves her in spite of what she did, and with the money he has won he gives up his activities as a bookmaker.

This film, Jean's last, marked Gable's sixth and Lionel Barrymore third appearance with her.

With Frank Morgan

With Lionel Barrymore, Clark Gable,
and Walter Catlett.

With Clark Gable

What the critics said about

SARATOGA

Marguerite Tazelaar
New York Herald Tribune
   Jean Harlow's last picture, which opened yesterday at the Capitol, made this particular individual feel sad. Partly because of a still fresh memory of the gifted young actress's untimely death, but also because of certain significant lines, which as she voiced them seemed almost a premonition of disaster. Looking ill much of the time and striving gallantly to inject into her performance characteristic vigor and vibrancy, the result, in face of subsequent events, is grievous.

With Walter Pidgeon and Clark Gable

With Clark Gable

Her few brief glimpses of natural brilliance as a comedienne, such as when Mr. Gable hides under the bed while she entertains her fiancé, only seem to intensify the shadow hovering over her spirit and subduing it. *Saratoga* is, in a way, an obituary of a lovely person and a talented actress. . . . The picture is entirely Miss Harlow's, tragic as it has proved to be. And she is surrounded by a fine, loyal cast.

Time Magazine

Saratoga, written by Anita Loos and Robert Hopkins, is possibly Jean Harlow's best picture as well as her last. Glib, forthright, knowing and adroit, released last week to coincide with the opening of the 1937 season at New York's old spa, it investigates the lighter side of the serious sport of horse racing with as much good sense as good humor.